GET MOVING!

Girl Scouts of the USA

Chair,
National Board
of Directors

Connie L. Lindsey

Chief
Executive
Officer

Kathy Cloninger

Vice
President,
Program

Eileen Doyle

Girl Scouts®

WRITTEN BY Valerie Takahama

CONTRIBUTORS: Judy Gerstel, María Caban,
Amélie Cherlin, Cheryl Kushner,
Kathleen Sweeney, Christine Brongniart

ILLUSTRATIONS: Dez by Meghan Eplett, comic
by Sarah Oleksyk, infographics by Melinda Beck.

DESIGNED BY Alexander Isley Inc.

EXECUTIVE EDITOR, JOURNEYS: Laura Tuchman

MANAGER, OPERATIONS: Sharon Kaplan

MANAGER, PROGRAM DESIGN: Sarah Micklem

Photographs

Page 15, from top: ©2008 Courtesy Energy
Retail Association, UK; ©2008 Nicky Bonne;
©2008 Courtesy Studio 804/University
of Kansas; **Page 40**: by Brian Augustine;
Page 50: Mark Thiessen/National Geographic
Image Collection; **Page 54**: NASA/courtesy of
nasaimages.org; **Page 64**: California Academy
of Sciences photos courtesy of Charmagne
Leung; **Page 65**: Hufton + Crow/courtesy of
Sheppard Robson; **Page 67**: by Cheryl Muhr;
Page 73: courtesy of the Bren School of
Environmental Science & Management; **Page
82**, from left: AP Images/Kyodo News; courtesy
of Mazda Motor of America; courtesy of Antro;
Page 103: BLOOMimage

**This Girl Scout journey is funded in part
by Trane, a business of Ingersoll Rand
that is working to make a difference in
energy efficiency around the globe by being
a world leader in heating, ventilation, and
air-conditioning systems and services. For
more information, visit www.Trane.com.**

Text printed on Fredrigoni Cento
40 percent de-inked, post-consumer fibers
and 60 percent secondary recycled fibers.

Covers printed on Prisma artboard FSC
Certified mixed sources.

Mixed Sources
Product group from well-managed
forests and other controlled sources
www.fsc.org Cert no. SQS-COC-100209
© 1996 Forest Stewardship Council

CONTENTS

Off the Charts, Off the Grid — 4

Investigate Your Spaces — 60

You, Unplugged — 14

On the Move — 76

Waste, Energy, and Wasted Energy — 26

¡Vamos Ya! — 85

Energy Insights from Wilderness and Wildlife — 44

Energy Award Tracker — 106

Why Light the Night Away? — 54

Moving Right Along! — 111

Off the charts, Off the GRID

All of these use energy. {
TVs
blow dryers
iPods
microwaves
planes
trains
automobiles
places
spaces

ENERGY
makes things

Energy makes the wheels on a bus go 'round. It's also what picks you up when you fall down.

Energy makes you go. It also helps you think, breathe, dream, and grow. It can get you going when you feel low.

Energy is what makes animals go, too. It keeps birds soaring in the sky, monkeys swinging in the trees, and horses running wild and free.

It gives you and the buildings all around you heat in winter and cool air when you need it, like in the movie theater on a muggy summer afternoon.

It's the same with all our stuff and things. Someone forgot to recharge the cellphone battery? Then it won't work. Didn't turn on the washing machine? Then the dirty clothes won't get clean.

Leadership is all about energy too. A leader knows how to use her own energy to motivate herself and everyone around her. A leader uses her energy to care for Earth's energy.

Or maybe a storm downs a power line? The electricity goes out and that's it— until work crews arrive to make repairs.

Energy plugs into so much of life. But we tend to take it for granted—until it stops.

People all around the world are becoming aware that some serious repairs are needed to how we use our energy resources. We're using too much of it and that affects everything on Earth: insects, plants, animals, and you!

Did you skip breakfast? Haven't eaten any protein yet? Then you've got no get-up-and-go to get you through your day.

You can use your personal energy to protect all the awesome things on this planet. And you can use your energy to make better use of energy— everywhere in your life.

On this journey, you'll investigate energy all around you:

- **the energy inside you**
- **the energy in all your places and spaces**
- **the energy of getting from here to there—everywhere you go.**

Wise use of energy brings its own reward—greener, healthier living! It also brings Girl Scout awards. Three awards are offered on this journey. You can earn one, two, or all three. Just look for the award icons:

And follow all the steps in your

ENERGY TRACKER

on pages 106–109. You'll notice that if you do go for all three, and you put them together like so,

you'll get a special energizing effect to power you through all your future Girl Scout adventures and leadership efforts.

Your path to these awards will also have you lightening your energy load. As you unplug from the energy grid, you'll plug into something bigger: nature. Go outdoors, take a walk in a park, or camp in the wilderness. Take time to see how plants, insects, and animals use and conserve energy.

Say,

Ciao bella!

to Dez, the fashionista spider who's taking this journey with you. Dez always has something to say. She's full of energy! Did you know that spiders spin webs so they don't have to run after their prey? That helps them save energy. And then they eat their webs to get back the energy they spent making them. How's that for recycling?

Energy—yours and the planet's—and how to use both wisely in all you do: That's a lot of what this journey is all about.

But this journey is also about you—how to realize your energy, increase your energy, and enjoy every bit of energy you can each day as you tackle all the energetic things you do, including fun stuff. That's what *Get Moving!* is all about.

So what are you waiting for?

GET MOVING!

Energy is the ability to do work. It's what's needed to move things from one place to another or to change things from one form to another. There are two basic forms of energy: kinetic energy and potential energy.

Kinetic Energy

The energy of motion, whether waves, wind, atoms, electrons, or objects, like a swing or a jump rope.

Thermal Energy, or heat, is also kinetic energy. It's the internal energy in substances. The thermal energy of food is increased when it is heated on the stove. The stove's heat is transferred to the soup and the internal energy of the soup increases.

Electrical Energy is the movement of electrical charges. Electrical charges moving through wire is called electricity. Lightning is also electrical energy. Lightning occurs when there is a discharge of electricity, frequently between clouds and the ground.

Radiant Energy is the energy of electromagnetic waves, such as visible light, x-rays, and radio waves. Solar energy from the sun is also radiant energy.

Sound Energy is the energy of waves traveling through air and other materials that we interpret as sound. Bang on a metal pot, and the vibrations set up waves that enter our ears.

Ride the wave
We see the color red when light waves bounce off an apple. We hear music when sound waves shake our eardrums. Our bodies turn high-calorie milkshakes into heat waves. Gamma rays from exploded stars pass through us like we aren't even here. See where your human energy fits into the cosmic flow.

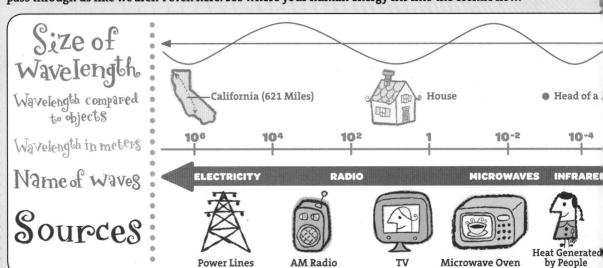

Size of Wavelength

Wavelength compared to objects
California (621 Miles)   House   ● Head of a

Wavelength in meters 10^6 10^4 10^2 1 10^{-2} 10^{-4}

Name of waves   ELECTRICITY   RADIO   MICROWAVES   INFRARE

Sources
Power Lines   AM Radio   TV   Microwave Oven   Heat Generated by People

Potential Energy

Stored energy that is ready to be used and changed into another form. A stretched rubber band has potential energy. So does a roller coaster at the top of the track. They both have the potential or the ability to change without any added energy; the rubber band can shrink to its original size and the roller coaster can coast down the track.

Chemical Energy,

the energy that is stored in the bonds between atoms, is potential energy. A battery has potential energy to make electrical energy to run a CD player or TV remote control.

Stored Mechanical Energy is another type of potential energy. It's the energy stored in objects that came from an applied force. Squished and stretched springs have stored mechanical energy.

Gravitational Energy, like that in a sled at the top of a hill, is a third type of potential energy. So is the energy in water held behind a dam. When water from a dam flows downhill, that's the energy of hydropower.

Nuclear Energy is also potential energy. It's the energy in the nucleus of an atom that holds the nucleus together. When nuclear fission happens, the nucleus splits into smaller parts, giving off lots of energy.

Virus   (h) Water Molecule

-6 10^{-8} 10^{-10} 10^{-12} 10^{-14}

ULTRAVIOLET   X-RAY   GAMMA

isible Light   X-Rays   Radioactive Elements

How's Your ENERGY?

Do you have potential energy stored up inside you? What are your hidden potentials that are ready to help you achieve your goals?

Measuring ENERGY

Check out your lightbulbs and see how many watts they use. W is short for watts. A 60 W bulb means that if you use it for one second, you use 60 J of energy.

Remember, k means 1,000. So, using a 60 W lightbulb for one minute uses 3.6 kJ of energy.

Suppose you use a 60 W lightbulb for one hour. Then you use 216,000 J of energy. By the way, one BTU is about 1,055 joules. So, if you found one thing telling how many BTUs it uses and another telling how many joules it uses, you could figure out some way to compare the two of them.

A **calorie** is the word we use when we talk about the amount of energy in food. But what we call a calorie is really 1,000 calories. The short way to write this is 1 kcal; k is the shortcut for 1,000 in the metric system and cal is short for calories. (As you learn to save energy on this journey, you may find yourself burning a lot of calories because you're using more of your own energy!)

A **joule** is another way we talk about amounts of energy and it is frequently used when talking about electrical things. A joule, written as J for short, is equal to one watt of power working for one second.

BTU, or British thermal unit, is a basic unit of thermal energy. It's the amount of heat needed to raise 16 ounces of water 1 degree Fahrenheit. BTUs are used to tell us how much heating and cooling our furnaces and air-conditioners can do.

Energy We Use Every Day

- Pick a room that you know. Draw a diagram of it.
- Place an X in 5–10 places where energy is used in the room.
- Then label those places with the kind of energy taking place.

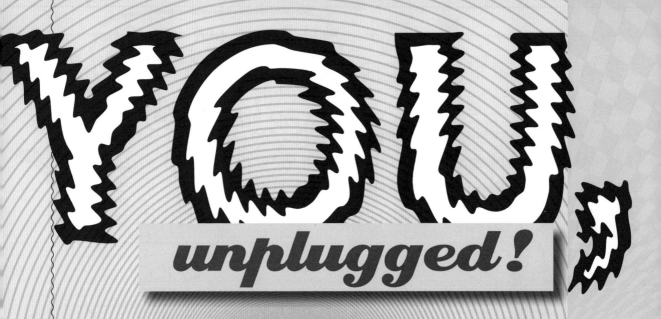

YOU, *unplugged!*

The world is abuzz over energy use

The way we use energy can have big consequences. One of them is called global warming, and it's just what it sounds like. The average temperature of Earth's atmosphere is rising bit by bit because we're burning too much gas, coal, and oil. We're using too much nonrenewable energy!

Rising temperatures cause glaciers to melt, oceans to rise, and animal and plant species to become extinct.

But there's good news, too. If we act wisely and swiftly, the hope is that global warming can be halted, maybe even reversed. In fact, good changes have already begun. Throughout the world, people are developing ways to use the sun and wind and water as energy. These environmentally friendly energy sources don't cause Earth's temperatures to rise.

Right now, government leaders are enacting laws to reduce carbon emissions, the leading cause of global warming. And ordinary people in communities around the world are taking action to reduce their "carbon footprint," one measure of their impact on the environment.

The residents of the villages of Hove and Brighton in England have reduced their carbon footprint by half. And they did it using small measures like switching off lights, adding insulation to their homes, and paying attention to "smart meters," which sound an alarm when electricity use gets too high.

On the island of Samsø in Denmark, the roughly 4,000 residents have shrunk their carbon footprint by 100 percent—and they did it in just five years! They use wind power to produce electricity, and solar and biomass energy (fuel from plant materials and animal waste) for heating.

After a devastating tornado ripped through their small rural town in 2007, the 1,400 residents of Greensburg, Kansas, decided to rebuild as a model green community. Now their homes will be 50 percent more energy-efficient, businesses will run on solar power, and all public buildings will meet the highest environmental standards.

What's Your Carbon Footprint?

Your carbon footprint is a measure of your impact on the environment. It's the amount of greenhouse gases emitted by all you do. Greenhouse gases trap too much of the sun's energy in the Earth's atmosphere and this contributes to global warming. A carbon footprint is measured in units of carbon dioxide (CO_2).

What kinds of things contribute to your carbon footprint? Driving in a car, using a computer, and eating a hamburger. It takes energy to do all these things: gas to power the car, electricity to run the computer, electricity and gas to process and transport the hamburger.

Watching TV for two hours or driving a car for a mile will add a pound of CO_2 to your footprint. If you lower your footprint, you do less harm to the planet.

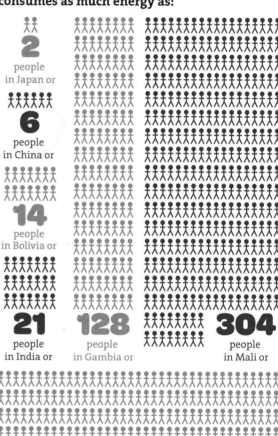

The Juice on Energy Use

On average, one person in the United States consumes as much energy as:

2 people in Japan or

6 people in China or

14 people in Bolivia or

21 people in India or

128 people in Gambia or

304 people in Mali or

478 people in Afghanistan

1750 **Year**   1800   1850

A World View

How CO_2 emissions compare, by country, as a percentage of total world emissions

China 20.6%
Total CO_2 emissions
in million metric tons: 6,018
Population: 1,330,044,544

United States 20.2%
5,903
303,824,640

Russia 5.8%
1,704
140,702,096

India 4.4%
1,293
1,147,995,904

Japan 4.3%
1,247
127,288,416

Using the numbers given, can you calculate the average emissions per person in each country?

China _____

United States _____

Russia _____

India _____

Japan _____

■ Total CO_2 emissions in million metric tons　　■ Population

Now, how would THAT work for me? Do I GET 3 carbon footprints?

Up, Up, and Away!

This graph shows how CO_2 emissions have risen steadily over time. Years are along the bottom, CO_2 levels along the side.

Sources: The Juice on Energy Use and A World View: figures on energy consumption and carbon emissions (from consumption and flaring of fossil fuels), International Energy Annual 2006, U.S. Department of Energy; population figures, CIA World Factbook, July 2008. Up, Up, and Away: carbon emissions (from fossil-fuel burning, cement manufacture, and gas flaring), 1751-2005, Oak Ridge National Laboratory, Oak Ridge, Tennessee.

Global CO_2 Emissions (in million metric tons)

29,360
27,525
23,855
19,500
22,020
20,185
18,350
16,515
14,680
12,845
11,010
9,175
7,340
5,505
3,670
1,835
0

1900　　1955　1965　1975　1985　1995　2005

You may have heard the phrase "off the grid." It means living disconnected from the electrical power grid and going without other public utilities like water and natural gas. Living off the grid is a pedal-to-the-metal way to save energy.

NOW,
What *you* can do?

What do you think Dez should pledge?

Here's a challenge: Try going off the grid (or at least partway off!) for a day, a weekend, or a week. That means getting by without flipping a light switch or using any electrical appliances.

It means walking, biking, or sharing a ride wherever you go. It means no IMing, e-mail, or computer games. It means using natural light as much as possible, so it might also mean going to bed earlier than you're used to, and getting up with the sun!

Write your own energy pledge after talking with your family about what's doable and practical in your life right now. You might use the suggestions on the following pages as a start. Commit to all the pledge points, or some, or even just one. Or come up with your own based on your energy level! The point is to try something to save energy.

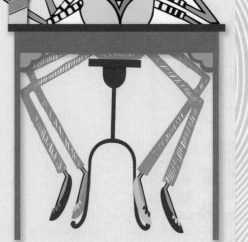

I will save energy by:

Not turning on lights. Use a hand-cranked flashlight or lantern (or a battery-powered one, if you must) to navigate. It's good practice for when you go camping!

Hanging up unsoiled clothes so they don't get wrinkled and need to be washed or ironed after one wear. And I'll use cold water to wash my clothes. About 90 percent of the energy used to wash clothes just heats the water.

Traveling on my own energy as much as I can. That means walking and bicycling when you can. Get your family to help with carpools, too!

Playing board games or reading by lantern light or making my own music. How many songs do you know the words to by heart? Practice card tricks. Look at the night sky and make a wish on a falling star.

Eating less meat. Livestock farming produces 18 percent of the planet's greenhouse gas emissions—that's more than cars emit. Be adventurous! Go beyond mac 'n' cheese.

Not turning on the TV or playing video games or using the computer except for schoolwork. And by unplugging electrical appliances when they're not in use. (Plugged-in electronics use energy even when not turned on.)

Talking with family and friends face-to-face, free of distractions (especially from gadgets).

Carrying my own reusable fork, knife, and spoon, and cloth napkin when I go out to eat. Disposable utensils add up! China uses about 45 billion pairs of wooden chopsticks per year—that's an annual loss of about 25 million trees.

19

MY ENERGY PLEDGE

I will save energy by:

Turning pff lights when I'm not useing them.

by not using lights when I don't need them.

Hey, Want a Real Energy-Saving Adventure?

See if your entire Junior Girl Scout team will gear up for a day or weekend off the grid—a real survival outing. Get moving!

Think About It

What did you learn while off the grid? What can you share with others about what you learned?

Living the Girl Scout Law

By following through on your Energy Pledge, you will be using resources wisely. That's living the Girl Scout Law! And you'll be living other values of the Girl Scout Law, too! Can you name those other values? Hint: There are at least three of them!

D onna Zimmerman uses fresh-picked vegetables from small New York farms to make the soups she sells at New York City farmers' markets. "Everything is seasonal," she says.

Donna's soups are also vegan, which means they're made without animal products—no meat, dairy, or eggs. The absence of dairy and meat extends the soups' shelf life and the use of unpeeled, organic vegetables boosts the vitamin content (a vegetable's nutrients are often concentrated in its skin).

Donna Zimmerman
SOUPS THAT ENERGIZE

"The cooking itself is energizing," Donna says. When customers hear the soups are vegan, "everybody lights up."

"Definitely learn to cook for yourself," Donna adds. These days, the Cleveland, Ohio, native, who was raised on TV dinners and tuna casserole, even whips up fresh food for her two dogs. The pups aren't vegans, but they do eat broccoli and brussels sprouts.

Donna rents a church kitchen just two blocks from her apartment, so she walks to her "food studio" and then transports containers of soup by subway to the market. All food scraps, and the biodegradable cups and spoons used by her customers, are composted at a community garden.

Donna is also working on a cookbook—on recycled paper, of course!

Recipe: **Any Bean Soup**

From: Donna Zimmerman

Serves: 6–8

1 pound dry beans
(black, red, navy, pinto,
or kidney beans)
2 carrots, chopped
1 stalk celery, chopped
5 garlic cloves, chopped
1 small onion, chopped

2–3 tablespoons olive oil
8 cups soup stock
(you can dissolve 2 bouillon
cubes in water to make the stock)
Sea salt and pepper to taste
(Optional: yogurt or sour cream for garnish)

Put beans in a large pot of water, making sure you have 2 inches of liquid above beans. Bring to a boil, then turn off immediately. Let beans sit for 2 hours. (Did you know that soaking beans removes the chemical that causes gas?)

Drain beans in a colander and rinse.

Chop carrots, celery, garlic, and onion. Empty water from the pot and put in vegetables. Add olive oil.

On low heat, cook vegetables for 10 minutes, or until onions are clear. Add beans and the soup stock. Raise heat to a boil, then cover pot, reduce heat, and simmer until beans are tender.

Remove pot from heat and let cool to room temperature.

Transfer beans and liquid to a blender or food processor and puree until creamy. (You may need to do this in small batches.)

Return pureed soup to the pot and heat on low heat until warmed.

Add sea salt and pepper to taste. Serve in bowls and enjoy!

Optional: Garnish each bowl of soup with a dollop of yogurt or sour cream.

Jenni Larmore's town needed a place where dog owners could exercise their pets and socialize, so she created one.

Paw Power Dog Park, in Clermont, Florida, spreads over four acres and is shaded by 100-year-old oak trees. The park's five sections accommodate dogs of all sizes and activity levels. Each area has an agility course and stations for drinking, waste, and washing.

To get started, Jenni surveyed pet shop owners, veterinarians, and dog owners about their needs and desires. She then presented a proposal to the Lake County Parks and Trails Department that included the concept, location, blueprints, projected costs, and a project work plan.

Jenni Larmore
PAW POWER
DOG PARK

"I am super-convincing when I really believe in something and can convey that to people when I speak to them," Jenni says.

And so, the work began.

Jenni enlisted members of the Girl Scouts of Citrus Council and recruited other volunteers through community bulletins. A perimeter fence was installed, the land was cleared of vines and debris, and brick pavers were laid to level the ground. Discarded fire hydrants and tires got new life in the park. A fund-raising dog wash paid for agility equipment.

Dozens of volunteers spent more than 136 hours over 13½ months to make Paw Power a reality. Even young Girl Scouts helped by spray-painting the decals that mark the park's various sections.

Jenni began her project in fall 2005 as an 11th grader. It won her a Girl Scout Gold Award and a 2008 National Young Woman of Distinction honor. Since then, she has spent many more "rewarding hours" working there.

An INNOVATIVE Idea
Pets and Parks

Is parkland for pets needed in your town? Do pet owners have a place to walk and talk and enjoy the fresh air and exercise?

A dog run is a great way to Get Moving on two (or four!) feet! Who would you contact to get a pet play space under way? Who might join your effort?

Going for Goals

When Jenni Larmore set out to create Paw Power Dog Park, she set two personal goals: to use time more efficiently and to be more organized.

Do you have any personal goals for this journey? Want to deepen your friendships? Do homework faster? Widen your network? Meet an engineer and shadow her for a day or two at her work? Write your goals here:

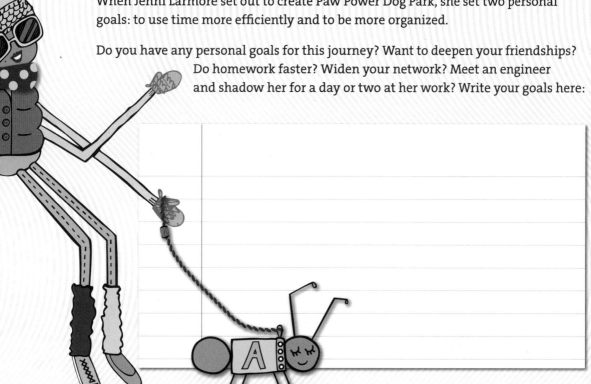

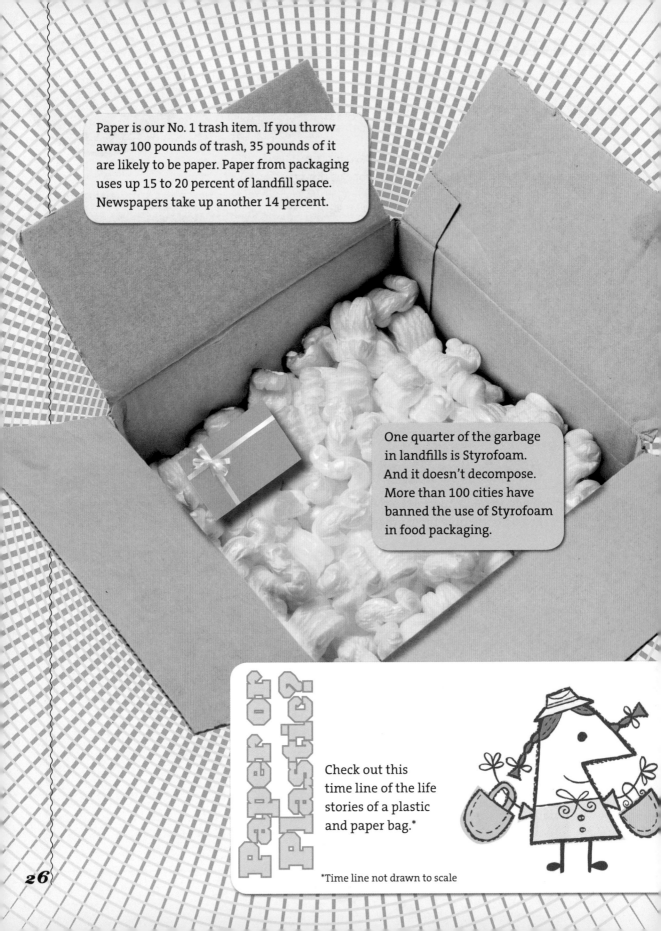

Paper is our No. 1 trash item. If you throw away 100 pounds of trash, 35 pounds of it are likely to be paper. Paper from packaging uses up 15 to 20 percent of landfill space. Newspapers take up another 14 percent.

One quarter of the garbage in landfills is Styrofoam. And it doesn't decompose. More than 100 cities have banned the use of Styrofoam in food packaging.

Paper or Plastic?

Check out this time line of the life stories of a plastic and paper bag.*

*Time line not drawn to scale

Waste, Energy, and WASTED ENERGY

Manufacturing paper requires a lot of energy and other resources. In fact, papermaking plants use more water than any other industry, and paper manufacturing is the third-biggest producer of greenhouse gas, after the chemical and steel industries. In the United States, it takes 12 percent of the nation's total energy use to manufacture all the cardboard, newsprint, paper towels, toilet paper, and other paper products that we use and then throw away.

251 million to 100 million years ago

The age of dinosaurs: Tiny sea organisms die and sink to the ocean floor, to be covered with sand and silt. Heat and pressure turn them into oil. Someday that oil will become a plastic bag.

27

Continued next page

Of course, it all starts with trees. The paper and wood products that each of us uses in a year equal a 100-foot-tall Douglas fir tree. *Tim-ber-r-r!*

Has your family ever ordered a new gizmo online or received a gift by mail and had it arrive wrapped in so many layers of packaging that it reminded you of one of those Russian doll sets? You know, the ones where a big doll opens to reveal successively smaller and smaller dolls nestled inside.

The dolls are lovely and fun to open, and certainly conserve space, but what about your package? When it comes, you open the outer layer that has the postage and the mailing address. Underneath is a bunch of cushiony packing material, or packing peanuts, surrounding another cardboard box! Open that, and you may face even more packing material before you reach the thingamajig you ordered, which has its own packaging made of cardboard and shrink wrap, or plastic, or tissue paper. Open that up, and, finally, there's your doodad— along with an instruction booklet, a warranty, and maybe even a catalog of more thingamabobs and doohickeys!

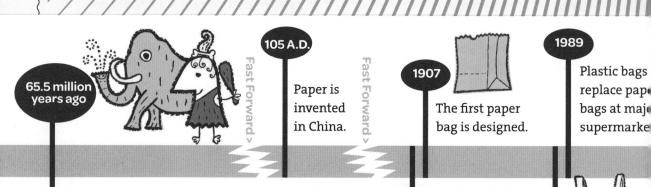

65.5 million years ago
The age of mammals begins when a big meteorite wipes out the dinosaurs.

Fast Forward >

105 A.D.
Paper is invented in China.

1883
Leo Baekeland invents the first all-synthetic plastic.

Fast Forward >

1907
The first paper bag is designed.

1977
The plastic grocery bag is invented.

1989
Plastic bags replace paper bags at major supermarkets

Even a roll of holiday wrapping paper comes in shrink wrap. And those colorful gift bags with the coordinated tissue paper you use so you don't actually have to wrap your friends' birthday presents? Chances are when you buy them at the store, you carry them home in—you got it—a paper or plastic shopping bag!

Luckily, not everyone thinks that more is better when it comes to packaging. For instance, one major toothpaste maker has done away with the cardboard boxes that toothpaste tubes usually come in. It did that by using stouter, more rigid tubes that can be shipped without damage and displayed upright on store shelves.

And it's not just the big players. An indie rock group has asked its fans and college groups to collect old CD jewel cases and send them in. The band members clean the cases and reuse them when they put out their own CDs. How green is that?

To make books sold in the United States each year, more than 30 million trees are cut down to create new paper. The book you are reading is printed on recycled paper.

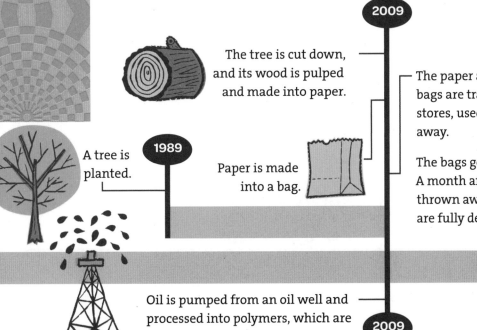

2009
The tree is cut down, and its wood is pulped and made into paper.

The paper and plastic bags are transported to stores, used, and thrown away.

A tree is planted.

1989

Paper is made into a bag.

The bags go to a landfill. A month after being thrown away, paper bags are fully decomposed.

Oil is pumped from an oil well and processed into polymers, which are heated and pressed into plastic bags.

2009

Natural Packaging

Collectors believe Russian nesting dolls originated in Japan, where they represented *Shichifukujin*, the seven gods of good fortune and happiness. When the Japanese dolls reached Russia around 1890, they became *matryoshka* dolls, a term derived from *Matryona*, a popular woman's name at the time. The root of the name is *mater*, or mother, so the dolls are often associated with motherhood.

There's also a connection between the dolls and things in nature. Think of an onion and all its peelable layers. Take away one layer and you have a smaller but still perfect onion.

Next time you're outdoors, or in a food market, count all the nesting and natural packaging shapes you can find. Peas in a pod? Nuts in a shell? Fava beans with their pod and shells? Cloves of garlic? Start a contest with friends. See who can find the most natural nestings.

I found these natural nestings:

3010?

No one is sure how long it will take the plastic bag to decompose. Scientists' estimates range from 500 to 1,000 years.

A Doll of a Recipe

The first *Junior Girl Scout Handbook*, published in 1963, featured a recipe for Walking Salad for One. Read it below. How could you transform it into a "Russian Doll" salad to carry on a hike on a cool day? Hint: Skip the mayo, and use cubed cheddar or another firm cheese instead of cottage cheese (mayo needs refrigeration; ditto on cottage cheese, which can also get runny and messy on a hike). And don't mix the ingredients together. Nest them one after another inside the cored fruit. Fruit, cheese, and nuts—that's a snack chock-full of energizing protein, carbohydrates, and fiber!

Recipe: Walking Salad for One
From: Girl Scout Handbook
Serves: 1

1 apple
2 tablespoons cottage cheese
5 or 6 raisins
2 or 3 nuts, chopped
1 teaspoon mayonnaise

Cut the top off the apple.

Core the apple almost all the way through, leaving the bottom skin intact.

Scoop out the pulp and chop it up with cheese, raisins, and nuts.

Mix with mayonnaise.

Stuff the mixture in the apple shell and put the top on.

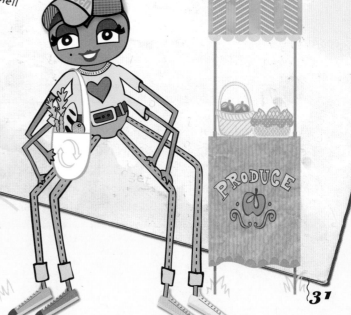

Paper or Plastic?

Bring your own reusable shopping bag!

ENERGIZE

Weighing a Week of Waste

Try this: For one week, collect all the paper and packaging materials that you would normally throw away—boxes, Styrofoam trays, plastic and paper containers, egg cartons, wrappers, too. Collect cans, jars, plastic wrap, and cardboard. Don't forget the junk mail, newspaper, magazines, and writing paper.

How high a stack do you have? Measure it! Now separate your stack into two stacks—items that can be recycled and those that can't be. How much of your waste can be recycled?

Get Creative with Cutbacks

When a major fast-food chain switched from foam containers to paper wrapping, it reduced its packaging volume by more than 70 percent. That meant big reductions in energy use! So look again at your stack. Which items would you trim back? How would you redesign them to make them less wasteful?

Mission: Decomposition

How long will the trash in our landfills take to decompose?

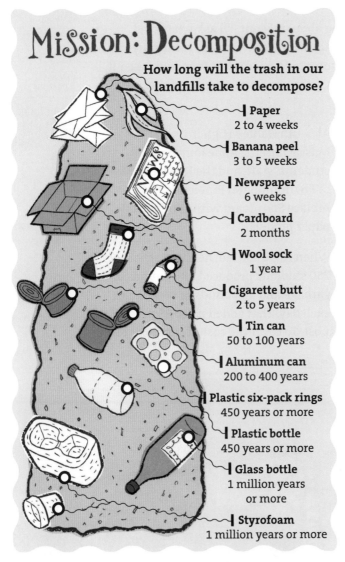

Paper
2 to 4 weeks

Banana peel
3 to 5 weeks

Newspaper
6 weeks

Cardboard
2 months

Wool sock
1 year

Cigarette butt
2 to 5 years

Tin can
50 to 100 years

Aluminum can
200 to 400 years

Plastic six-pack rings
450 years or more

Plastic bottle
450 years or more

Glass bottle
1 million years or more

Styrofoam
1 million years or more

Paper or Plastic... Money

Paper bills sometimes get pretty grubby. And they tear, too. Can you imagine using plastic money? Australia, Mexico, and Brazil already do!

Cool Recyclables

Did you know that some toothbrushes and razor handles are made from yogurt cups? Here are some more second-generation goods.

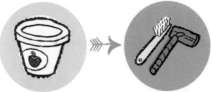

yogurt cups → toothbrushes and razor handles

takeout containers → cutting boards

potato chip bags and juice cartons → handbags

old sweaters → rugs

a fighter plane → a hotel (it's in New Zealand)

plastic bottles → fleece jackets

"If I go out to a restaurant and I'm thinking about takeout, I'll ask what kind of containers they use," says Abbe Hamilton. "I'm not willing to contribute to the Styrofoam problem anymore." Commonly used for fast food and takeout, Styrofoam has been known to litter beaches, parks, and waterways around the world.

Abbe Hamilton
SAYING **NO** TO
STYROFOAM

At South Hadley High in Massachusetts, Abbe joined with students, staff, and the Department of Environmental Protection to replace Styrofoam with compostable paper products.

When Abbe started, her high school of 750 students produced 135 pounds of garbage and 20 pounds of recyclables each day. That added up to 85 percent garbage, 15 percent recyclables, and no compost. To cover the cost of compostable plates and cups, Abbe applied for and received a state grant. Now plates and cups are mixed with food waste and transported to a farm to be combined with manure and eventually sold as fertilizer.

After one year, her school's six bags of daily trash were reduced to two bags, and the daily garbage pickup was cut to once a week. Total garbage was reduced by 66 percent! The cafeteria waste is now 40 percent recycling, 35 percent compost, and just 25 percent garbage.

Abbe's project earned her a Girl Scout Gold Award and the honor of being a 2008 National Young Woman of Distinction.

An INNOVATIVE Idea
How Does Your School Cafeteria Rate?

How's the waste situation in your school cafeteria? INVESTIGATE! Are disposable plates and cups being used? What are they made of?

If they're not compostable, can you get your principal and cafeteria staff on board to go green? Who might join you in your effort?

Abbe Hamilton's experience offers some good ideas for starting a composting project at your school.

Here are Abbe's tips:

1 Trust your enthusiasm.

2 Find a supportive teacher. Science teachers can help you explain why it's so important to reduce waste.

3 Make friends with the custodial and cafeteria staff. Learn what bins they currently use. Be polite and respectful, and approach them when they're not in the thick of lunchtime!

4 Projects take time, planning, and commitment, so networking is key! Form an environmental club and seek out professionals who can help locate resources, like donated compost bins.

5 Can your school use the compost? If not, consider starting a school garden. Remember: It takes about a year to make compost.

6 To spread the word, make fliers from recycled materials, or use text messages or e-mail.

7 Schedule student monitors during lunchtime to keep the compost bins free of trash.

Be Prepared to Sell Your Idea!

No matter how innovative your idea, you'll need to be prepared with facts about how your project can have a positive impact.

"Be Prepared" is the Girl Scout motto. If you want a project to succeed, be prepared for any questions that might come your way! What facts did you learn from Abbe's project that could help sell the idea of reducing cafeteria waste at your school?

How about making some of your own Recycled Paper?

Get creative with your ingredients. It'll be even more fun if you try it with friends.

What You'll Need:

A piece of screen, such as a window screen, or a papermaking screen and frame

Recycled paper—tissue paper, newsprint, printer paper, wrapping paper, envelopes—ripped into small pieces (about a half-inch square)

Recycled or natural decorative bits (optional)—ribbons, threads, fabric, postage stamps (be imaginative!), leaves, grass—snipped into small pieces

Plastic basin for water runoff

Electric blender

Rags (lots) and 1–2 old towels

Newspapers or old tablecloth

Butter knife

Pieces of cardboard cut to match the size of your screen

Step 1: This is a fun but messy job, so set up your workspace with newspapers or an old tablecloth. You might want to put some newspapers on the floor as well. And wear old clothes!

Step 2: Place the screen on top of the plastic basin. If the screen does not have a frame, tape it to the basin top.

Step 3: Fill your blender ⅔ full of warm water and fit into base. Sprinkle in 1–2 handfuls of torn paper. Let soak for at least 30 minutes.

Step 4 (optional): Arrange decorative bits on screen, facedown.

Step 5: Secure blender lid (very important!), and turn blender on low. Water may leak a bit, so have rags ready. Allow to spin for 30 seconds. Paper pulp should look like clouds and have the consistency of oatmeal. Immediately lift out the blender container and bring it to your screen. Pour quickly through your screen.

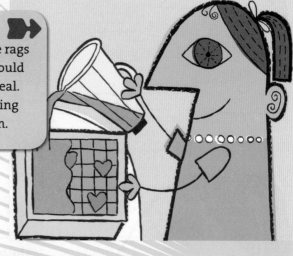

Step 6: Use precut cardboard rectangles to gently press excess water through the screen, then lift the cardboard off (you may need to use the butter knife to pry the pulp page from the cardboard). Make sure most of the water is pressed out, then flip the screen over onto an old towel or tablecloth. The paper page will detach from the screen. Leave to dry.

Voilà! You've made your first handmade page of paper from recycled materials! Now make another one! If you don't like uneven, bumpy edges, place another towel over your fresh pages and put a heavy book on top to weigh them down.

Paste a sample of your handmade paper here:

Paper Pleasures

Making recycled paper uses fewer resources and creates less pollution than making new paper.

And we're using more recycled paper than ever. In 2007, 56 percent of the paper used in the United States was recycled. That equals more than 360 pounds of paper for every person in the country.

ENERGIZE GS

What did you enjoy most about making paper with your Girl Scout friends?

Keep a tally of all the things you're able to do with your handmade recycled paper.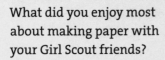

I used my handmade recycled paper to:

Now that's using resources wisely!

Did you know that paper can be made from weeds, sunflowers, cattails, carrot tops, and the little brown stems on banana peels? Akua Lezli Hope, an artist and writer in upstate New York, makes paper out of all these and more.

Akua grew up in Harlem in New York City, where she was a Girl Scout. "We were poor, but I always had crayons and paper and tools. And I was always told, 'You can do anything you want to do.' "

Akua was always very creative, playing the bassoon and cello, singing in choruses, and writing poems and stories, which used lots of paper. "And then I fell in love with the paper itself," she says.

At first, Akua used shredded paper to make papier-mâché for sculpting. But then she focused on making paper and started experimenting. After all, most paper comes from trees, so why not use plants, especially those that might otherwise go to waste, to make beautiful, handmade paper?

Akua Lezli Hope
PAPER FROM NATURE

"Wild growing things make fantabulous paper," she says. "Cattail heads make dark brown paper that looks like leather. Silkweed paper is glossy and golden and strong. The outer skin of the milkweed makes a great resilient paper."

For Akua, paper is the most satisfying expression of her creativity. "Paper appeals to so many senses," she explains. "It appeals visually and to the sense of touch and the sense of smell. And when you've made a good piece, it's crisp and you can hear it. You feel it and you can use it."

It would probably be best if the world just stopped making plastic bags. Until then, Cindy Endahl, aka Recycle Cindy, is turning them into hard-wearing fashion purses and chic messenger bags.

How does she manage that? With imagination, a crochet hook, and a ball of yarn—make that "plarn," yarn made from one-inch strips of ordinary plastic shopping bags that are knotted together.

Cindy uses 12 to 15 bags to make a mini shoulder bag and 45 to 50 to create a large tote. It takes her one to five hours to complete a project, depending on how large and complicated it is.

Cindy is a deputy clerk in Newport, Washington. One day she spotted a woman with an unusual crocheted bag on her arm and learned that it was made from plastic shopping bags. An avid crocheter since she taught herself a few basic stitches as a girl, Cindy set out to make one of her own.

Cindy Endahl
AKA RECYCLE CINDY

She not only mastered the technique and made herself a cute bag, but she created new styles of handbags and dreamed up other plarn items, like baby bibs, coasters, and water bottle holders. She started posting the patterns for her creations on myrecycledbags.com in 2006.

Imagine one-of-a-kind fashions made from 75 percent trash. That's right, trash! Soda cans, plastic grocery bags, old phone books, junk mail, even rusty nails and salvaged car parts are transformed into elegant gowns, cocktail dresses, and other garments.

One evening gown, made from 12,000 pieces of crushed recycled glass and leftover upholstery material, is glittery enough for the Oscars. A backless cocktail dress has shimmering fringe made from aluminum cans. The dress itself was a shower curtain!

Like real high-fashion gowns, these are hand-sewn and take up to 400 hours to make.

The designer behind this Recycle Runway collection is Nancy Judd. She came up with the idea for a "Trash Fashion" contest while working as an administrator in recycling for the city of Santa Fe, New Mexico, in 2000.

A cocktail dress of old canvas and rusty nails, with matching hat, purse, and shoes.

Nancy Judd
RECYCLE RUNWAY

"In fashion, there is huge waste when you consider how frequently clothes are discarded," Nancy says. "I'm striving to change the way people think about the environment through changing the way they think about waste."

Her garments have been commissioned by major corporations and the entire collection has traveled the country as an educational art exhibit.

Nancy learned to sew as a child. As a college student, she noticed that a garbage receptacle near a soda machine was filled with aluminum cans. She got permission to place a recycling bin nearby, which led to an independent study in recycling methods.

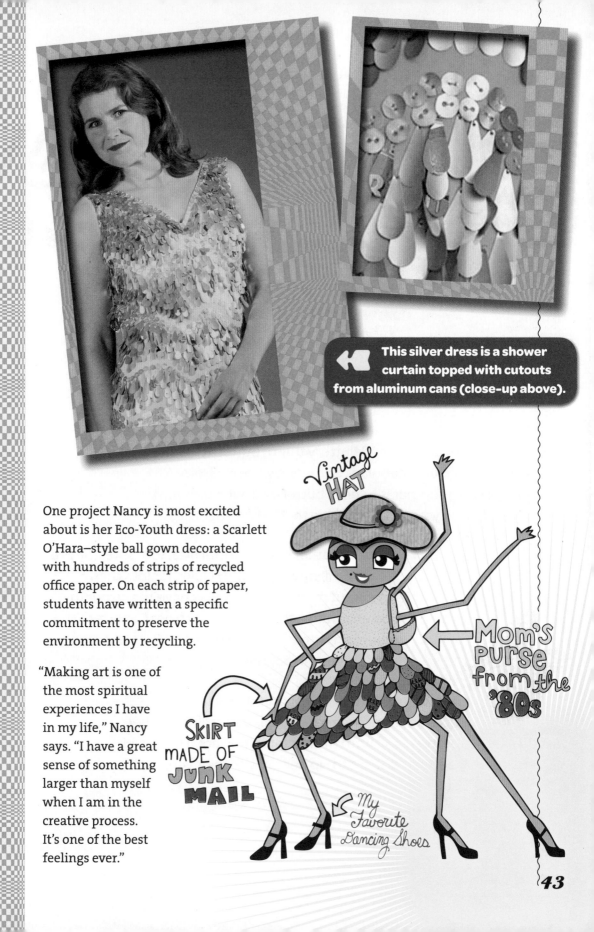

This silver dress is a shower curtain topped with cutouts from aluminum cans (close-up above).

One project Nancy is most excited about is her Eco-Youth dress: a Scarlett O'Hara–style ball gown decorated with hundreds of strips of recycled office paper. On each strip of paper, students have written a specific commitment to preserve the environment by recycling.

"Making art is one of the most spiritual experiences I have in my life," Nancy says. "I have a great sense of something larger than myself when I am in the creative process. It's one of the best feelings ever."

Vintage HAT

Mom's Purse from the '80s

SKIRT MADE OF JUNK MAIL

My Favorite Dancing Shoes

43

ENERGY

insights

From Wilderness and Wildlife

What's more delicate and fluttery than a butterfly? It's even part of our vocabulary. Someone who flits from one party to another is a social butterfly. That nervous, jittery feeling you get before a big test? That's right, it's the butterflies.

There's another side to butterflies, too. Sure, they're small and lightweight—they weigh far less than a dime—but monarch butterflies have the strength and endurance to fly all the way from Canada to the mountains in central Mexico, a 3,000-mile journey. That's energy in action!

Each one of the millions of butterflies that makes the trip is an energy marvel in itself. Butterflies get their fuel primarily from the nectar of flowers. They reach deep into flowers to sip nectar with their very own feeding tube.

The monarch butterfly's migration takes several months, during which up to four generations of butterflies are born and live out their life span. Even the newest butterflies know the route to Mexico.

Global Warming and Migration

Rising temperatures cause ice to melt, the seas to get warmer, and deserts to spread, which can have devastating consequences for all types of animals, including those that migrate. For example, arctic terns have been showing up later than expected in their migrations due to climate change forcing them to change their routes and also messing with their food chain.

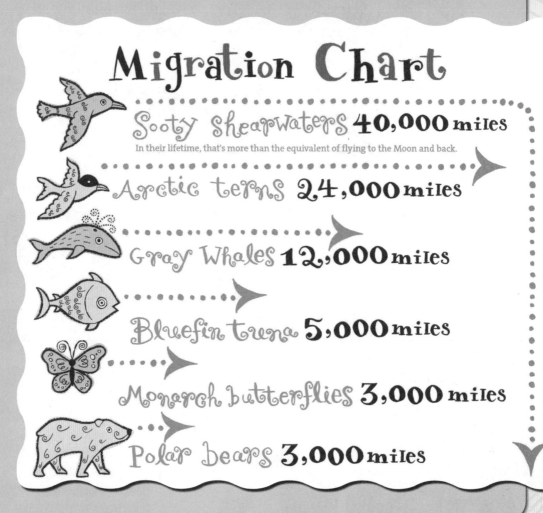

Migration Chart

Sooty Shearwaters **40,000** miles

In their lifetime, that's more than the equivalent of flying to the Moon and back.

Arctic terns **24,000** miles

Gray Whales **12,000** miles

Bluefin tuna **5,000** miles

Monarch butterflies **3,000** miles

Polar bears **3,000** miles

To fly properly, butterflies need a body temperature of at least 80 degrees Fahrenheit. Like snakes and lizards, they're cold-blooded. They can't create heat inside their bodies like humans and birds do. They depend on their surroundings to raise their body temperature. That's why you sometimes see butterflies sitting on rocks or high in trees basking in the sunshine. They're using solar energy to keep warm.

When the temperature dips too low, they have a hard time flying at all, which makes them easy prey for predators. Some butterflies have wing patterns that help them blend into their environment, or markings meant to look like the face of another creature in order to scare predators away. Brightly colored wings can warn birds and other predators that the butterfly is foul-tasting or poisonous.

Monarchs begin their migration in August. It's believed that changes in light and temperature tell them when it's time to leave. They feed along the way and store fat in their abdomens.

Butterflies are cold-blooded, energy-efficient, & incredibly ♥ beautiful—just like ME!

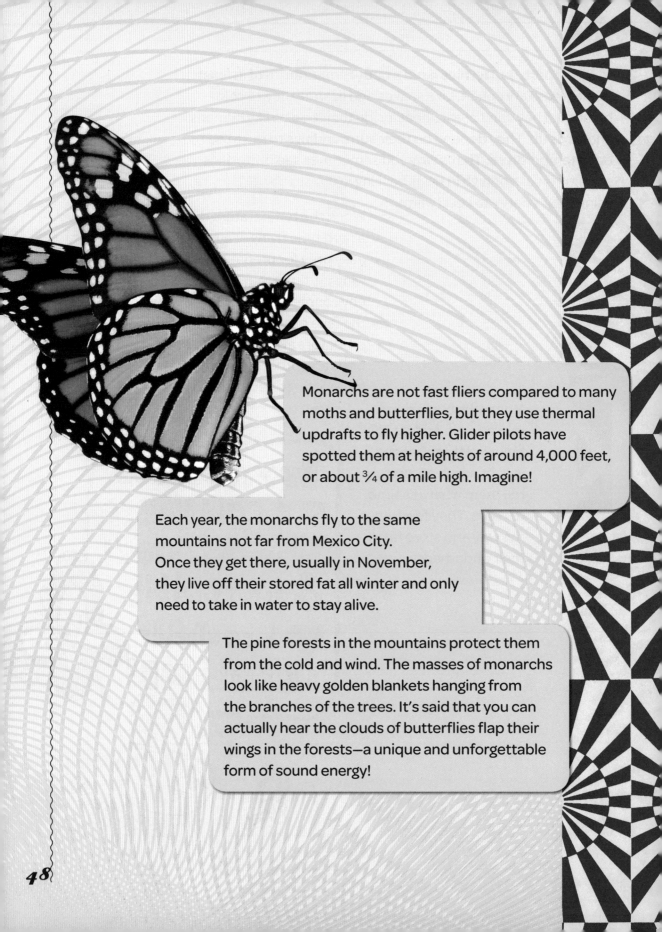

Monarchs are not fast fliers compared to many moths and butterflies, but they use thermal updrafts to fly higher. Glider pilots have spotted them at heights of around 4,000 feet, or about ¾ of a mile high. Imagine!

Each year, the monarchs fly to the same mountains not far from Mexico City. Once they get there, usually in November, they live off their stored fat all winter and only need to take in water to stay alive.

The pine forests in the mountains protect them from the cold and wind. The masses of monarchs look like heavy golden blankets hanging from the branches of the trees. It's said that you can actually hear the clouds of butterflies flap their wings in the forests—a unique and unforgettable form of sound energy!

Stomp in a Rain Puddle!

Have you ever noticed how cheerful you feel after playing outdoors? There's something calming and energizing about walking or running or just moving in nature. Maybe it's the fresh air. Maybe it's got something to do with endorphins or some other chemicals in the body. Whatever it is, we like it! Here are some things you can do outside. Which do you enjoy most? Add your own, too! Do one (or more) and it will count toward your ENERGIZE award!

1 walk the dog

2 jump in a pile of leaves

3 bodysurf

4 build a snowman

5 sled down a hill

6 fly a kite

7
8
9
10
11

Remember the shiny-eyed, long-tailed "party animals" from the movie "Madagascar"? Those were lemurs. Mireya Mayor studies lemurs in the wild. And she has a lot in common with them.

Lemurs rely on their agility to leap acrobatically through the rain-forest canopy. As a primatologist working in the rain forest, Mireya draws on her experience as a ballet dancer and a cheerleader for the Miami Dolphins.

"Having danced ballet for so many years actually helped me get around the rain forest," she says. "You need a lot of balance and flexibility, and you need to be very quick on your feet."

Mireya Mayor
DANCING THROUGH THE RAINFOREST

In college, Mireya took an anthropology course. Right away, her curiosity was piqued. In 1996, she went to Guyana in South America to study primates. Mireya, who had never even been camping, found herself clambering through jungles, trying to avoid "snakes and tarantulas that would somehow appear on my backpack!" A year later, in Madagascar, Mireya and a colleague discovered the world's smallest primate, the pygmy mouse lemur. It weighs less than an ounce. Mireya's efforts led Madagascar to triple its protected regions and established a $50 million conservation fund.

Be Prepared!
Be Open to Using What You Know in More Than One Way

How has something you've learned prepared you to do something else entirely different?

What else do you want to be prepared to do in your life?

50

D o you like big animals? Scientists and conservationists have a term for animals that people seem to like enough to want to save from extinction. It's "charismatic megafauna," or "charismatic species." The giant panda, the tiger, and the blue whale are charismatic species.

So is the Asian elephant.

As manager of a conservation lab at the Smithsonian National Zoological Park in Washington, D.C., Melissa Songer tracks the movement of Asian elephants. It's important work because Asian elephants face extinction. Only about 30,000 of them remain in the wild.

Melissa Songer
ELEPHANT WATCH

Elephants can get down steep, muddy hillsides better than humans or machines, so Melissa and her team use them for transportation during the rainy season in remote parts of Myanmar, in Southeast Asia. "They just have this incredible balance—it's amazing what they can do," she says.

Asian elephants are also astonishingly dexterous. "They can pick up tiny little things with their nose 'fingers,'" Melissa marvels.

Being so big, Asian elephants need a lot of energy to move around. But they eat low-energy foods such as roots, grasses, fruit, and bark. So they consume up to 300 pounds of food each day over as many as 18 hours! To find that much food, they must move around a lot.

Elephants can run faster than people, but they usually conserve their energy and move slowly. Being big, they don't have to worry about predators. "There's not much that can mess with them," Melissa says.

Energizing sights Around

The northern lights, or **AURORA BOREALIS**, have awed people in northern latitudes for eons. These spectacular, unpredictable light shows are caused by ion particles from the sun entering Earth's magnetic field on gusts of solar wind. Spiraling and colliding with molecules of oxygen, nitrogen, and hydrogen, they create a breathtaking visual effect of ethereal gold, green, red, or purple.

The source of Nepal's longest, largest river, the **KARNALI**, is high in the highest mountains in the world, the Himalayas in Tibet, at a place that Hindus and Buddhists believe is the center of the universe. When the snows melt, the river runs fast through steep canyons and gorges, and past lush jungle vegetation and sandy beaches.

the World

One of the world's top surfing spots, the **GOLD COAST** of Queensland, Australia, is a magnet for beginning surfers, pros, and anyone who's energized by crystal-clear waters, crashing waves, and more than 50 beaches.

The local name for the spectacular **VICTORIA FALLS** in Southern Africa is Mosi-oa-Tunya or "the smoke that thunders." The falls are twice the height of New York State's Niagara Falls. Their mist is visible from miles away. Victoria Falls also boasts one of the richest displays of plants and wildlife of any waterfall site in the world.

Why LIGHT the night away?

Chances are you know the nursery rhyme "Star light, star bright, the first star I see tonight..." But did you also know it's becoming harder to see the stars at night?

Hundreds of years ago, even just a few decades ago, people could see many more stars than we can today. That's because we're using more and more streetlights, housing lights, and bright lights outside buildings and in parking lots, sports stadiums, and shopping malls. It's a problem just like water pollution and air pollution. Can you guess what it's called? That's right, light pollution!

Earth at night: a color-enhanced image made of hundreds of night-time photos taken by satellites that detect all kinds of light, from city lampposts to lightning.

55

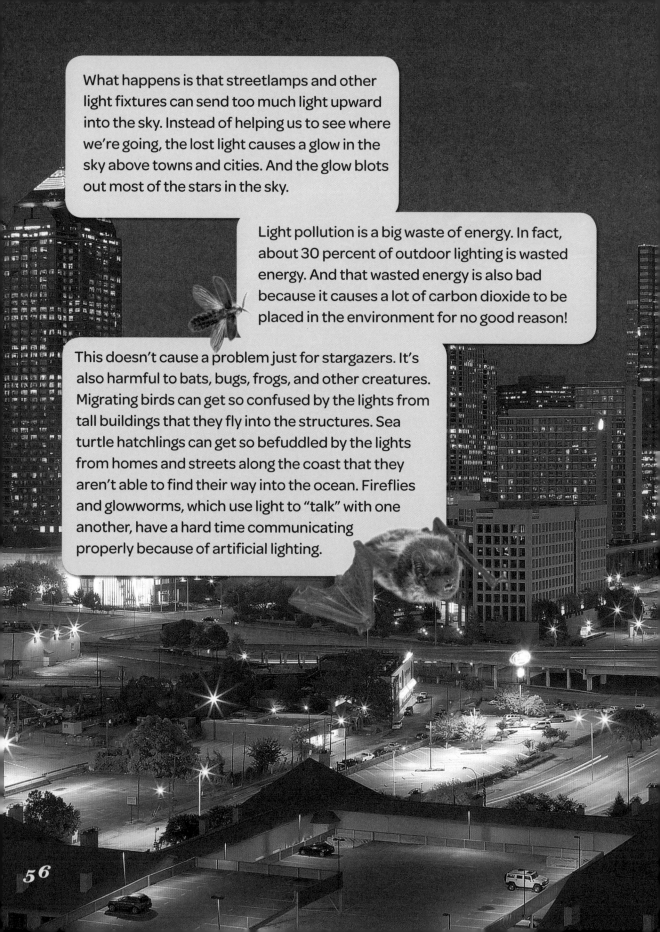

What happens is that streetlamps and other light fixtures can send too much light upward into the sky. Instead of helping us to see where we're going, the lost light causes a glow in the sky above towns and cities. And the glow blots out most of the stars in the sky.

Light pollution is a big waste of energy. In fact, about 30 percent of outdoor lighting is wasted energy. And that wasted energy is also bad because it causes a lot of carbon dioxide to be placed in the environment for no good reason!

This doesn't cause a problem just for stargazers. It's also harmful to bats, bugs, frogs, and other creatures. Migrating birds can get so confused by the lights from tall buildings that they fly into the structures. Sea turtle hatchlings can get so befuddled by the lights from homes and streets along the coast that they aren't able to find their way into the ocean. Fireflies and glowworms, which use light to "talk" with one another, have a hard time communicating properly because of artificial lighting.

But the picture isn't all dark. Astronomers began shedding light on the problem as far back as 50 years ago. Scientists at the Lowell Observatory, near Flagstaff, Arizona, helped get the city to keep the skies dark at night by banning advertising searchlights. Since then, they've been joined by environmentalists, lighting designers, and others who've helped spread the word about light pollution in communities around the globe. It's known as the dark-sky movement and it encourages cities and businesses to use streetlamps and other fixtures that send light to the right places.

"No dark-sky advocate is saying we want to make the entire city dark. No, no, no," says Connie Walker, an astronomer with the National Optical Astronomy Observatory, in Tucson, Arizona. "They're saying, let's light up the city wisely. Let's use the correct fixture. Let's use the correct wattage. Let's use the right number of fixtures, and [put] light where we want light, and not . . . where we don't want light."

That helps to keep the first star light and all the stars bright!

And that's using resources wisely.

How Dark Is Your Night?

Go into a dark closet, shut the door, and experience complete darkness. Go outside at night, and see if there's a difference.

In the wilderness, don't turn on your flashlight the moment you leave your car or go outside the tent. Let your eyes adjust to the dark, and you might be able to make your way without it.

Native Americans had lots of stories about the stars. The Shoshone tribe in Wyoming and southern Idaho had one about the Milky Way. They said a grizzly bear (the constellation Cygnus) climbed the mountains to hunt in the sky and got ice crystals stuck in its fur. As it crossed the sky at night, the ice fell off and became the Milky Way.

One of the most famous paintings in the world is Vincent van Gogh's "Starry Night." Look at how he depicted the stars at night.

What do you want the night sky to look like?
Draw it, collage it, write it!

When the Sun Goes Down and the Stars Come Out . . .

Go outside and look around. What lights are on? Where do they shine? What do they light up? How much light is wasted? Look up at the sky. Try to pick out the constellations. Can you find Orion? The Big Dipper? How bright are they?

Register Your Sky's Light with GLOBE at Night

Each year for two weeks in March, people in 110 countries measure the light in their cities' night sky and report their findings to a central location. The data from the GLOBE at Night campaign shows what areas of the world are brightest, and how those areas may be changing from year to year. The goal is to heighten awareness of the amount of light in the night sky. Want to take part? Visit the GLOBE Web site, globe.gov/GaN/.

The constellation Orion

A building in New Mexico made of adobe, which keeps homes cool in hot climates.

Wind catchers (also called wind towers), like the ones atop the Madinat Jumeirah Hotel in Dubai, have been used in the Middle East since ancient times to cool buildings.

Amanda Hall/Robert Harding World Imagery/Getty Images

Investigate Your SPACES

Energy in Buildings & Building for Energy

People are coming up with ways to renovate and build homes, stores, offices, schools, and other structures so they will use less energy and fewer resources. This is important because buildings account for about 40 percent of all energy use.

Plus, heating, cooling, lighting, and running buildings are responsible for 38 percent of the world's carbon emissions—that's more than comes from all the cars on the road. So buildings with energy-efficient systems and "green" buildings are best for the environment.

And there's a twist to this cool new trend. You've heard the saying "Everything old is new again"? Well, some of the ideas behind "green" buildings have been around for ages.

Yurts, tepees, and other tent-like structures have kept people sheltered from the elements for thousands of years. They're made from natural materials, such as wood, wool, and animal skins. Green builders often use natural materials, too—ones that can be easily recycled and don't have to be shipped long distances. These include straw bale (bricks made from stalks of wheat, rice, and other plants) and rammed earth (layers of compacted clay and sand).

Another natural building material is mud bricks, or adobe. It's one of the oldest building materials in the world. It was used by the Egyptians and other ancient civilizations in the Middle East and North Africa.

The ancient Anasazi people used adobe and wood to build villages on hilltops in the Four Corners region of what is now the American Southwest. They also made sure their dwellings faced south. That way, the sun shone directly into their homes in the winter for warmth and light. In the summer, the sunshine was shaded by overhangs that kept the homes cool. That's what's known today as taking advantage of a building's site to make use of passive solar power. Old ideas are suddenly new again!

Smart Growth

Where buildings are built is just as important as what they are made of. That's because a building's location can have a huge impact on energy use. A good way to save energy is to reuse older buildings or to build on empty lots within a city, town, or suburb. This creates walkable communities where people live close to stores, offices, schools, libraries, and public transportation. That means fewer cars on the road and more energy savings!

Dream Up Your Dream Green Home

Suppose you were an architect in charge of designing a dream green home. What would it look like?

Would it be nestled in a meadow and use a green roof to blend in with the landscape and also to insulate the building and reduce heating and cooling costs? Or would it be a U-shaped apartment building with a garden in the middle where everyone grew flowers and organic vegetables?

Or would you build it out of adobe in the desert and design a solar heating system for the swimming pool?

Or would it be a string of funky beach cottages with a wind turbine to make electricity from the sea breezes? When you decide, draw or piece together a picture of what it would look like. If you're an aspiring architect, go all out and make your image 3-D!

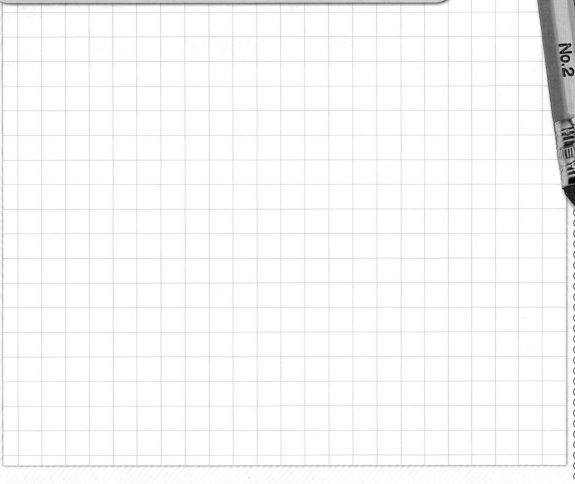

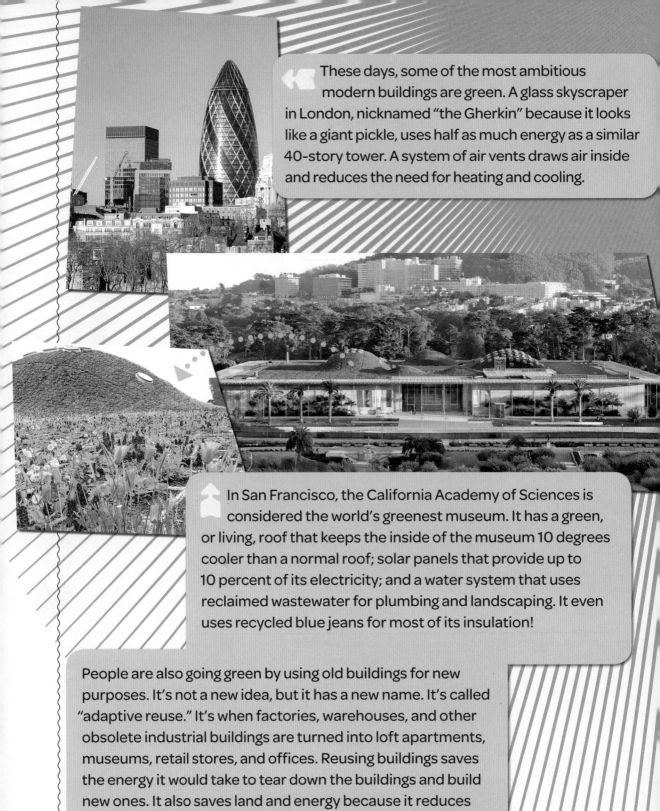

These days, some of the most ambitious modern buildings are green. A glass skyscraper in London, nicknamed "the Gherkin" because it looks like a giant pickle, uses half as much energy as a similar 40-story tower. A system of air vents draws air inside and reduces the need for heating and cooling.

In San Francisco, the California Academy of Sciences is considered the world's greenest museum. It has a green, or living, roof that keeps the inside of the museum 10 degrees cooler than a normal roof; solar panels that provide up to 10 percent of its electricity; and a water system that uses reclaimed wastewater for plumbing and landscaping. It even uses recycled blue jeans for most of its insulation!

People are also going green by using old buildings for new purposes. It's not a new idea, but it has a new name. It's called "adaptive reuse." It's when factories, warehouses, and other obsolete industrial buildings are turned into loft apartments, museums, retail stores, and offices. Reusing buildings saves the energy it would take to tear down the buildings and build new ones. It also saves land and energy because it reduces urban sprawl. Plus, old buildings often have a history and architectural features that make them worth preserving. It would be a shame to tear them down and lose their charm!

Schools are going green, too. They are being upgraded with energy-efficient heating, cooling, and control systems, and water-saving devices. When possible, they make use of large windows and skylights to let in natural light, and roof overhangs to block the sun's heat. These features save money and create a better learning environment. Studies show that students perform better when in a comfortable environment, one that's quiet, has clean air, and uses natural light.

Many people believe that in the future, most buildings will be eco-friendly.

How does your school rate?

A Real Power House!

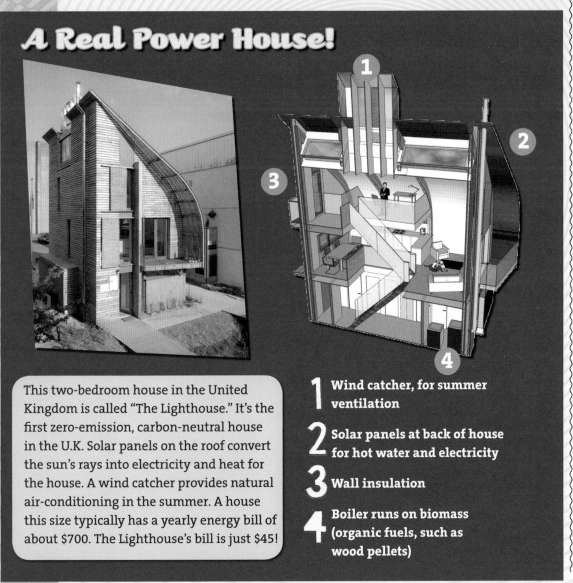

1 Wind catcher, for summer ventilation

2 Solar panels at back of house for hot water and electricity

3 Wall insulation

4 Boiler runs on biomass (organic fuels, such as wood pellets)

This two-bedroom house in the United Kingdom is called "The Lighthouse." It's the first zero-emission, carbon-neutral house in the U.K. Solar panels on the roof convert the sun's rays into electricity and heat for the house. A wind catcher provides natural air-conditioning in the summer. A house this size typically has a yearly energy bill of about $700. The Lighthouse's bill is just $45!

An INNOVATIVE Idea
New Life for Old Digs

Can you identify an old, empty building in your town or city that could be turned into something else? What could it become? An art museum? A community center? A school? Draw a picture of the building as it is now, and one of it as you imagine it to be. Find out who owns the building and ask them what their plans are for it.

Here's another idea: Is there a space or place in your school or in your parents' workplace that is unused or underused? Why not see if you can convert it into a pop-up art gallery? Fashion designers and retailers are setting up pop-up shops to call attention to their wares. You could borrow the idea to display your artwork and plans about smart energy use, and invite your classmates or your parents' coworkers to view them. And you can create a guest book—from recycled paper, of course—where people can leave their own comments and ideas!

Sarah Susanka is an architect and a writer. She loves solving problems. When she was a 10-year-old growing up in England, her teacher gave the class a puzzle to solve: Without taking your pencil off the paper, and using only four straight lines, connect the dots shown below.

Sarah spent hours working the problem. She knew there had to be an answer, yet she couldn't find it. Can you?

One night, Sarah awoke with the answer clear in her mind.

"What I discovered was that, if I stayed within the box created by the dots, I couldn't solve the problem," she says. "Once I broke the confines of the outline, the problem solved itself."

Her "thinking outside the box" led her to found the Not So Big movement, which has been embraced worldwide for its philosophy of building better, not bigger, houses.

Sarah Susanka
MAKING HOUSES
NOT SO BIG

Sarah's home in Raleigh, North Carolina, built in 1977, is an example of what she calls "tightening up energy-efficiency." She made the house less leaky by replacing the insulation and installing an energy-efficient heating and cooling system.

Such simple changes, along with energy-efficient lights, are a "big part" of saving energy today, Sarah says.

Energy Audit
Begin with a Bio

Buildings have biographies, just like people. For starters, they have a birth date—the year they were made. That gives you an idea of what kind of materials were used to create the building. Buildings might also have a record of when various parts were "retrofitted" to make better use of energy, like by getting a new heating or lighting system.

A building's bio also includes what kind of building it is—commercial, industrial, governmental, or a school or library—who owns and maintains it, what the electric and heating bills amount to each month, and who uses the building and how and when they use it.

All this information can help you think about how the building can be more energy-efficient. Can the lights be turned down more often? Who or what controls the air-conditioning and heating? Are the controls set properly? What are the monthly bills? Would a new heating, cooling, or building control system be more efficient?

GET MOVING!

Still here?
Together with your Junior teammates and your trusty adult, find a building and investigate its energy use. Take a tour with someone in charge of running the building. Who knows, you may be able to suggest some energy improvements!

INVESTIGATE

Be Prepared for Your Energy Audit!
Give Your Home a Green Once-Over

To get ready for the energy audit you and your Junior friends will perform, start with a wide-ranging visual energy audit of your home. Look for leaky windows, and lights and electrical equipment (computers, DVDs, stereos, kitchen equipment) left on or plugged in overnight.

What might you suggest your family do to be more energy efficient? Call a family meeting to discuss ways to save energy, such as:

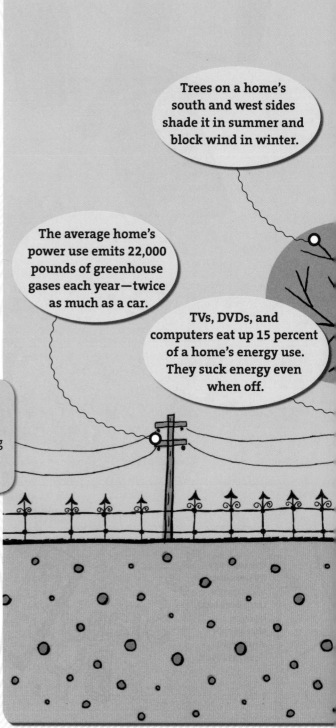

Trees on a home's south and west sides shade it in summer and block wind in winter.

The average home's power use emits 22,000 pounds of greenhouse gases each year—twice as much as a car.

TVs, DVDs, and computers eat up 15 percent of a home's energy use. They suck energy even when off.

Top Ways to Be Energy Smart

- Use a heating/cooling system with a programmable thermostat
- Plant trees for shade
- Use ceiling fans instead of A/C
- Keep drafts/leaks in check
- Use energy-smart lighting and appliances
- Replace old water heaters

Star Power!

Energy Star is a government-backed international rating system for energy-efficient consumer products. Appliances awarded the Energy Star seal use 10 to 50 percent less energy than standard appliances. How many Energy Star appliances can you find in all the buildings in your life?

Cutting the Bill

Get everyone in your home to cooperate for an entire month on cutting back the use of electricity. Compare your home's electricity bill before and after and write down the results. If electricity is included in your rent, ask your building manager to compare the bills and let you know the results.

1 An open door wastes as much as 25 percent of a store's total air-conditioning use. In New York City, it is illegal for stores to leave their doors open when air-conditioning is running.

2 A leaf blower runs on gas or electricity; a rake just needs your muscles!

3 A bucket placed in the shower or outside during a rain shower can collect water that can be used to water plants!

My Home Energy Sources

Electricity in my home comes from (coal-burning power plant, hydroelectric power, nuclear, solar power, other?)

Heat in my home comes from (electricity, gas, propane, wind or solar power, other?)

Now, Look at All the Buildings in Your Life

Once you've made an effort to green your home, take a wider look. Does your school, library, community center, or place of worship have windows that let in light and warmth in winter?

Do these buildings have shade protecting them in summer?

To be truly green, what are these buildings missing? What more might they need?

A quick visual audit will help you prepare for your full building audit with your Junior team. Use the Building Bio and Building Audit pages (74–75) to gather as much information as you can. Report what you find to the building's manager, along with your recommendations for how to be more energy-efficient. Using resources wisely is living the Girl Scout Law!

How Green Is Your School?

If you and your sister Juniors conduct an energy audit of your school, you may be on the way to some mighty energy savings. Why?

Schools are often some of the most energy-inefficient buildings in a community. Each year, taxpayers spend $6 billion on energy for schools, 25 percent of which could be saved through simple conservation measures.

Bren Hall at the University of California's Bren School of Environmental Science & Management was the first laboratory building in the United States certified LEED Platinum, the highest level of certification by the U.S. Green Building Council. It has a white-cap roof to reduce heat gain and a natural ventilation design that takes advantage of Pacific breezes. Its lighting uses as much daylight as possible and monitors lighting based on actual room usage.

My Building Bio

Building name:

Year built:

Operating hours:

Main use:

Other uses:

Number of people using it:

Type of HEATING and/or COOLING systems used:

Energy source for heating:

Energy source for cooling:

Energy items needing attention:

Broken windows (cracked, don't open, don't close)?

Drafts?

Poor insulation?

Window shades to block cold and/or heat?

Awnings or trees for natural cooling?

My Building Audit

My Junior team investigated the _____ building.

We thought it was very interesting that

One way to save energy in this building might be to

We talked to _____ who is in charge of _____ here.
We learned

and we suggested

I think auditing buildings is important because

Now that I know more about how buildings run, I might like to

On the MOVE

Biking WALKING carpooling & MORE!

Whee! What's more fun than riding a bike with the sun on your face, a breeze in your hair, and the scenery flying by? Whether you're pedaling hard or just coasting, bicycling can make you feel happy to be alive. It's a good way to get places. It's good exercise. And it's good for the environment.

Cars and light trucks are responsible for a third of the carbon dioxide (CO_2) released into the atmosphere. A study by traffic engineers found that cars idling in traffic in Los Angeles and New York add about 7.5 tons of CO_2 into the environment every year—and they're not even getting anywhere!

A bike emits zero CO_2. Zip. Nothing. Nada.

So people around the world are making it easier to bike.

They're starting community bike-sharing programs with names like Velo'v in Lyon, France; Bicing in Barcelona, Spain; and Bycyklen (City Bikes) in Copenhagen, Denmark. The popular Velib' program in Paris, France, has tourists and Parisians zipping off to the Eiffel Tower, the Louvre, and other landmarks.

In fact, bicycling is free wheelin' 'round the globe with programs that are at the starting gate or up and running. These programs put bikes where people are likely to use them for short trips, and they offer them for free or for just a small fee. When done riding, people drop off the bikes where they got them or at another bike rack in the system.

Bike sharing got its start in the 1960s with programs that relied on the honor system. People could borrow bikes as long as they returned them. But too often the bikes were stolen or damaged. In the White Bicycle program in Amsterdam, the Netherlands, all the bicycles were stolen in less than a month.

The White Bike program in Portland, Maine, was modeled after Amsterdam's program. But its organizers put a modern spin on their smaller-scale program. Instead of relying on the honor system, they used bike locks and posted the combination on a Web site. The program had a lower rate of lost, stolen, and vandalized bikes.

Newer programs often require a deposit or a membership fee, and to reduce theft, they use smart technology like electronic locks and GPS-like tracking systems.

Some bike programs give away bikes or offer them at a discount to college students willing to leave their cars at home. The goal is to curb campus traffic congestion and reduce parking needs.

There's even a bike program at an art museum in Hoge Veluwe National Park outside Amsterdam. At the Kröller Müller Art Museum, visitors can hop on one of 1,700 white bicycles to tour the 26 miles of bike paths that wind through acres of surrounding woodlands, grasslands, and sand dunes. You might even spot deer and wild boar that live in the park. By the way, these bikes have no extras—no lights, no bells, no gears. They run on human pedal power alone.

On My Honor . . .

The Girl Scout Promise begins with those words.

Schools and other organizations around the world operate on the honor system, which is basically a way to run things based on trust and honesty.

When have you used the honor system? Does it really work? How would you design an honor system for bikes? What would it take to make it work?

An INNOVATIVE Idea
Get your town pedaling!

Want to get a community bike-sharing program rolling? Let the energy of others move you forward! Let people know you need three main things: bike donations, assistance with sprucing up the bikes, and good, secure locations for bike pickups and drop-offs.

Ask officials in your community what they think of your idea. Gather names and contact information from people as you go. Here are some details to consider:

DO SOME WHEELING AND DEALING

Lots of people, and bike shops, have old bikes gathering dust. So ask for donations. Find some adults who can help you collect them.

PUT IT IN GEAR

Find places where people are likely to use bikes, and make those your pickup and drop-off sites. Do any shop owners have space or bike racks? Or start small, at your school.

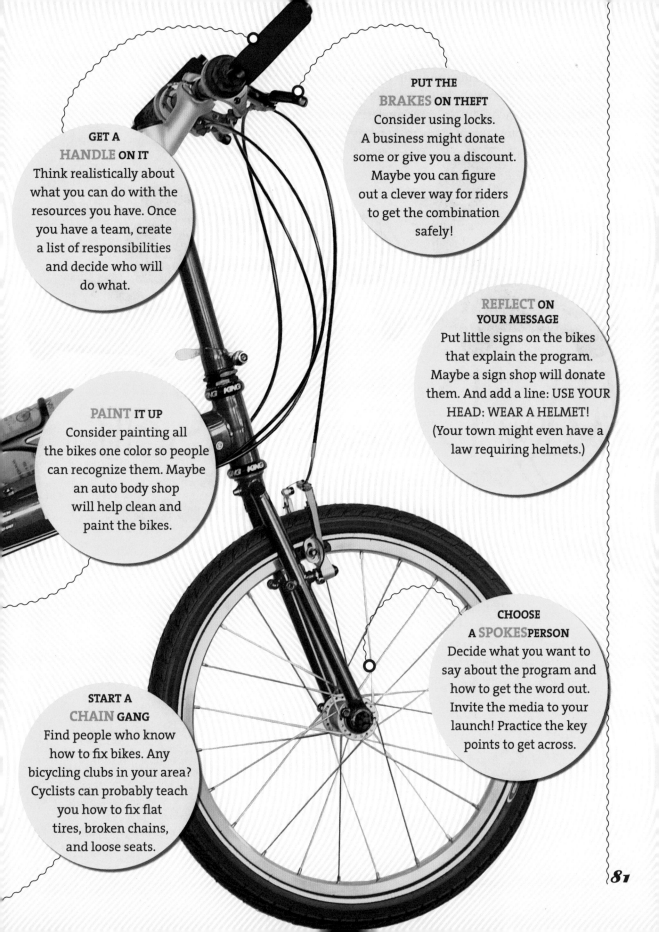

GET A
HANDLE ON IT
Think realistically about what you can do with the resources you have. Once you have a team, create a list of responsibilities and decide who will do what.

PUT THE
BRAKES ON THEFT
Consider using locks. A business might donate some or give you a discount. Maybe you can figure out a clever way for riders to get the combination safely!

REFLECT ON
YOUR MESSAGE
Put little signs on the bikes that explain the program. Maybe a sign shop will donate them. And add a line: USE YOUR HEAD: WEAR A HELMET! (Your town might even have a law requiring helmets.)

PAINT IT UP
Consider painting all the bikes one color so people can recognize them. Maybe an auto body shop will help clean and paint the bikes.

CHOOSE
A SPOKESPERSON
Decide what you want to say about the program and how to get the word out. Invite the media to your launch! Practice the key points to get across.

START A
CHAIN GANG
Find people who know how to fix bikes. Any bicycling clubs in your area? Cyclists can probably teach you how to fix flat tires, broken chains, and loose seats.

Designers have been dreaming up "cars of the future" for nearly a century. Early designs were sleek and futuristic looking and focused on high-tech convenience features. Later models were spare and practical. Here are three of the most recent, and most energy-efficient, dream designs.

My Dream Car
What would your dream car look like? Sketch it here!

Imagine a car that will be able to travel 40 miles gas-free and emission-free. That's what Denise Gray is working on. Denise, an electrical engineer, is in charge of the battery that will power the Volt, a new electric car from General Motors. It can be recharged by plugging it into any electrical outlet.

If the trip is longer than 40 miles, Denise explains, "a small internal combustion engine will get you to your location so you don't have to worry about running out of power." The engine won't power the wheels, though, as it does in a traditional car. It will power a generator that recharges the batteries.

"I've always been fascinated with advanced technology and doing things differently," Denise says, "whether making transmissions or improving fuel efficiency or using the battery as an energy source."

Denise's interest was sparked while growing up in Detroit. "When I was in middle school, I had a teacher who told me I was really good in math and science and told me to go into engineering," she says.

Denise Gray
AN ENGINEER WITH A
CHARGE

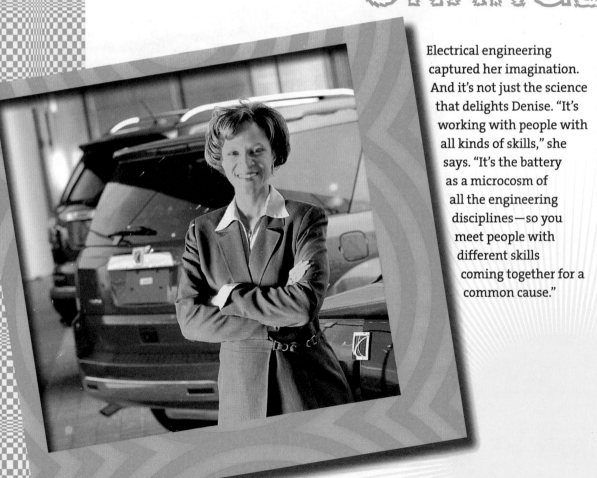

Electrical engineering captured her imagination. And it's not just the science that delights Denise. "It's working with people with all kinds of skills," she says. "It's the battery as a microcosm of all the engineering disciplines—so you meet people with different skills coming together for a common cause."

Robin Chase was at a café with a German friend in 1999 when she learned that in some German cities, people could rent cars for just a few hours. Robin realized that car sharing was a way to reduce pollution and also save money while still enjoying the convenience of a car when it was needed.

It was exactly what Robin needed, too. She grew up in Swaziland in Africa, where she was a Girl Guide, and was living in Cambridge, Massachusetts, with three children and her husband, who took the family car to work each day. "I wanted a car every once in a while for a few hours but I did not want to own one," Robin says. "The light bulb went off in my head."

Robin Chase
MAKING EACH CAR
COUNT

Most people drive their cars for only two of the 24 hours in a day, she explains. That's not using resources very wisely. Zipcar, the company Robin and her friend started, is now the largest car-sharing company in the world. "Zipcar is all about making efficient use of a car and conserving resources," she says.

Since the Zipcars are shared, each one is able to stand in for more than 15 cars that might normally be on the road.

Robin's newest venture is goloco.org. It's a ride-sharing network that lets people share travel plans via e-mail so they can share rides, too. Robin believes it's important for the environment "to get more people into the cars that are already on the roads."

Hey, slow down! Remind me, why'd we skip lunch?

To see the black jaguar.

That jaguar didn't growl nearly as loud as my stomach!

What's up?

ZOO

It won't start.

I think the battery's run down.

GROOOAN

That's how I feel.

Wake me when you get it fixed.

87

90

What's with the umbrella?

Sure. Let's get Megan, too.

We're going to Dillon Park—and making our own shade on the way! Want to come?

Expecting rain?

Very funny. Let's see how long you last in this sun.

Charlie, you look so silly. ¡Pobrecito!

¡Pobre pero bonito! Cute sunglasses! Are they designer?

WOOF! WOOF!

Woof-woof? Never heard of it.

He came home on his own! I guess he knows it's nearly dinnertime.

Oh, Charlie, you silly dog!

¡Qué día! What a day!

What a relief! How do you say that in Spanish?

You know, it was actually fun. I guess walking isn't so bad...

Walking is *good* for you! A 100-pound person can burn about 110 calories an hour walking.

I know it's good exercise. I guess I just don't like walking alone. I don't think it's safe.

I know what you mean.

So do I. It's weird.

Let's make a pact. When school starts, let's walk there together.

AWESOME!

FIRST DAY OF SCHOOL

I wish I could walk with them!

Hey, girls! Heading to school?

Yes! We have our own walking school bus.

I mean, it's not a formal one. We need an adult or two to make it official.

Right now it's just us.

And we love it!

What a great idea!

Let's take the walking school bus!

I want to take the walking school bus!

We'll check it out tomorrow. You can't be late on your first day.

cough cough

Hey, isn't that the cute guy from seventh grade?

You know, Americans use more than *400 million* gallons of gas each day! Wouldn't it be great if more kids walked to school? Think of all the gas we'd save.

And all the smelly fumes that wouldn't go into the air.

Let's get more kids on board our walking bus!

I know what we need to do...

A survey!

98

It'll never work.

Yeah. I was so psyched, but now...

No one was interested.

But we know it's a good idea.

Yeah, what about the kid from the treehouse?

And the woman with the garden?

And the cute guy?

Right. We can't give up just because we hit a little bump in the road.

Yeah. What if Susan B. Anthony had given up because everyone said that a woman's place was in the home and not the voting booth?

And what if J.K. Rowling had given up because the experts said, "Hogwarts to Harry, Hermione, and the rest. Write about something you know!"?

Yeah. And what if Steve Jobs had given up because the first iPod was as big as a backpack and only held one song?

What? That big? Only one song?

I don't know. But what if?

101

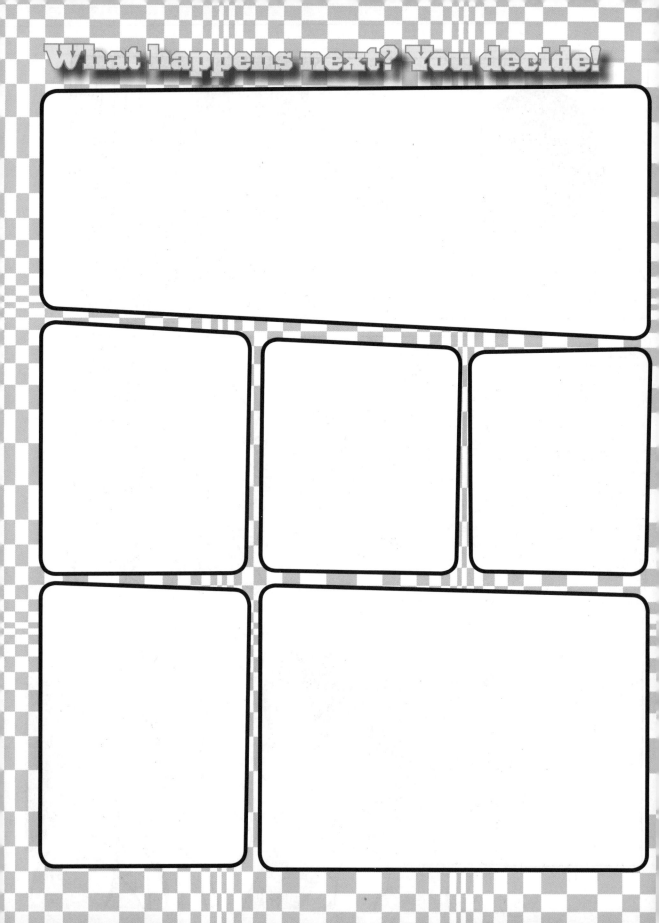

An INNOVATIVE Idea
All-H Aboard!

INNOVATE

More and more kids are riding the bicycle train or taking the walking school bus to school. Bicycle trains and walking school buses are fun—and they're good for the environment. All those cars idling outside schools dropping off and picking up students are wasting a lot of gas. Believe it or not, idling a car for only two minutes uses as much gas as it takes to go one mile.

Riding a bike or walking to school is also a good way to use—and recharge—your personal energy. It's good exercise. You might not know this, but fewer kids are walking or biking to school than ever before. In 1969, 42 percent of students ages 5 to 15 walked or biked to or from school. By 2001, less than half as many did. Even most students who live within a half mile of school don't walk or bike even one day a week!

One other thing:
Bicycle trains and walking school buses help ease people's worries about traffic and personal safety. There's safety in numbers—and there's an adult along for the ride!

Starting a small, informal bike train or walking school bus can be simple. It's as easy as getting neighborhood families to bicycle or walk together. Pick a route, recruit, and take a test run. Decide how many days a week the train or bus runs. And have fun!

My GET MOVING! Planner!

Traditionally, Girl Scout gatherings open with a ceremony, a game, or a song. These traditions connect you to Girl Scouts around the world and across generations. You can update old traditions or create new ones to pass on.

Got a song that would really get everyone up and moving? A game that will help your team work together better? Other ideas? Capture them here so you can share them with your team. It's going to be a great journey!

My Ceremony Ideas ....

....

My Game Ideas ....

....

Songs I Suggested ....

Energizing Snacks! Come up with your own ideas for
something good to make and share with your group. ....

....

Try something new at each Junior gathering that will relate to
ENERGIZE, INVESTIGATE, and INNOVATE.

Plan and prepare for the next gathering.

Closing Ceremony Ideas: Remember what was special about each gathering, and recognize your teamwork! Record the talents you and your Junior friends contributed.

Share your ideas! Check in with your adult volunteer and share ways to adjust plans for the next gathering based on your interests.

Something Really Special!

Maybe you'll go on a weekend campout or hike? Perhaps even as a big grand finale celebration. Maybe there is another energizing trip you want to take with your group. Jot ideas here and share with your team and, of course, your trusty adult. See what you decide on together.

How We'll Save Energy

Every time your Junior team gathers, try to use less energy. Can your families organize a car pool for drop-offs and pickups? How are you using your handmade recycled paper? What did you waste that you didn't need to waste? Candlelight ceremony, anyone? Get INNOVATIVE! It will ENERGIZE you!

ENJOYING how energized YOU FEEL?

ENERGY AWARD TRACKER

GS

No.2

Action	What Did You Do?	What Did You Learn?	How Can You Use It to Influence Others?
1 Make an Energy Pledge following the suggestions on page 19. Make it big or small, just make it doable for you.			
2 Try at least two other ENERGIZE activities suggested in this journey. Just look for the ENERGIZE icon. Some activities are about your energy and others are about the energy you use. Enjoying how energized you feel? Do them all—make them a regular habit!			
3 Check out all the ways that people are working on energy issues. Start with the women you meet in this book. Meet with someone working on energy issues in your community, maybe even an engineer. There are many kinds of engineers doing fascinating things. You might want to be one!			

ENERGY AWARD TRACKER

INVESTIGATE Your Spaces

1 Learn about energy use in buildings. Start with all the great information and diagrams right in this book.

What's the most interesting thing you learned? ....

....

....

2 Now use something you learned to work with your family to make one energy improvement in the building you know best, your home.

What did you do? How will this help? ....

....

....

3 Together with your Girl Scout group, INVESTIGATE the energy use in a building in your community—maybe your school, your library, your place of worship, or where your Girl Scout group meets. Be sure to talk to the people who run the building to exchange ideas. Use the diagram on page 71 and all the tips on pages 68–73 to decide what you will ask about.

What building did you visit? What did you learn? ....

....

....

4 Based on your visit, choose one way that you think the people who run this building could improve its energy use. Share your idea with them. Your adult volunteer will have some ideas to help.

What's your suggestion for how this building could run better? Who did you tell?

....

....

....

....

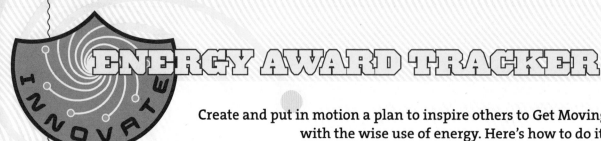

ENERGY AWARD TRACKER

Create and put in motion a plan to inspire others to Get Moving with the wise use of energy. Here's how to do it:

1 With your Junior friends, identify an energy issue in your community that needs an innovative solution!

Hint: Check out all the "Innovative Idea" sections in your journey book, and the comic story, too. Is anybody doing something about paper waste at your school? Organizing a walking schoolbus or bicycle train? Carpools? Shutting down some lights at night? Make a team decision: Choose an issue you will act on together.

What's your issue? ....

....

....

2 Research! Talk to two people (or more if you like) who might know something about your chosen issue or have an interest in helping you with it.

Hint: If you want to do something in your school, you might need to talk to the principal or members of a parent group . . . or . . . ?

If you want to organize a group to walk together a few days (or even just once) a week, you might start with your parents. Who else could help? Members of a local walking club, perhaps?

Who did you talk to? What did you learn? ....

....

....

3 Now that you have some ideas, develop your plan. Hint: You know, figure out specifically who will do what, when.

What's your plan? ....

....

....

....

....

4 Carry out your plan. Hint: Stop and think a little (or a lot!).
Do you need to adjust anything? How does it feel to be making a difference?

....

....

....

....

5 Share the news! Hint: Who can you pass your efforts on to? Maybe they can pass it on, too.
That's more energy savings—for you and the planet.

Who did you tell? What can they do? Who can they tell? ....

....

....

....

....

6 Reflect and say thanks! Hint: Remember everyone you've met along the way and how
they've helped. And think a little about what you might do differently next time you
innovate.

What impact have you had? How do you know? ....

....

....

....

....

....

....

....

Moving Right Along!

You've investigated energy all around you:

⇒ **the energy you use**

⇒ **the energy in all your places and spaces**

⇒ **the energy of getting everywhere you go**

You've energized. You've investigated. You've innovated.

Maybe the buildings in your life are getting more energy-efficient. Maybe you are, too!

Maybe you've kicked off an innovative plan that has even more people on the move for energy.

You've seen how energy flows through everything on the planet and beyond, from the lowly glowworm to the night-light in your bedroom to the twinkling stars up above.

And you've learned about your personal energy and how powerful it can be—for protecting Earth and for doing all that you do.

With all this energy bouncing around, don't forget to take a minute to think about how you've been a leader.

What have you discovered about who you are and the values you stand for?

How have you connected with others on your Junior team and beyond?

How else can you use your energy to Take Action in big and small ways to make the world a better place?

Now **celebrate**—in an energetic way!

Or how about a truly energy-efficient party? Gather your Junior friends and start planning. The energy level is up to you!

Try to get an energizing discussion going!

Which parts of this journey challenged you the most?

Which are you most proud of?

Now that you're picking up speed, you'll see there's so much more to accomplish. Be the engine of change. Continue to use your energy, and continue to inspire other people to use theirs. Together, the whole world can *Get Moving!* And that's something to celebrate.